Totally AMAZING FACTS ABOUT STUFF WE'VE BUILT

CARI MEISTER

CAPSTONE PRESS
a capstone imprint

TAJ MAHAL

Construction: 1631-1653

The Taj Mahal is a **BURIAL SITE**. It honors Mumtaz Mahal, Shah Jahan's third wife.

About 20,000 WORKERS and 1,000 ELEPHANTS worked on its construction.

Its HUGE CENTRAL DOME reaches a height of 240 FEET (73 meters).

The white marble walls seem to CHANGE COLOR throughout the day.

LOUVRE

Construction: 1200-2011

PARIS, FRANCE

The Louvre is one of THE LARGEST MUSEUMS IN THE WORLD. It has about 35,000 permanent art pieces.

It was once a **FORTRESS** and a **ROYAL HOME**.

ITS **FAMOUS PYRAMID ENTRANCE** WAS FINISHED IN 1989.

The pyramid is made up of almost 800 GLASS PANES.

THE "OLD" OAKLAND BAY BRIDGE

Construction:
1933–1936

SAN FRANCISCO, CALIFORNIA, USA

When the bridge was completed, it was the longest bridge ever built. It was 8.5 miles (14 kilometers) long.

ABOUT 167,100 TONS (151,591 METRIC TONS) OF STEEL ARE IN THE BRIDGE.

UNTIL 1962 CARS WENT ACROSS THE UPPER BRIDGE DECK. TRUCKS AND TRAINS WENT ALONG THE LOWER DECK.

THE "NEW" OAKLAND BAY BRIDGE

Construction: 2002-2013

SAN FRANCISCO, CALIFORNIA, USA

The new Oakland Bay Bridge is the world's longest self-anchored suspension span bridge.

Workers placed steel pilings for the bridge's base up to **300 feet (91 m)** below the water's surface.

Some of the bridge's beams CAN TWIST AND MOVE during an earthquake. The movement allows the bridge to stay stable.

MORE THAN 100 MILLION VEHICLES CROSS THE BRIDGE EACH YEAR.

ROME, ITALY

THE COLOSSEUM

Construction: about 70-80; modifications made 81-96

The Roman Colosseum is the **LARGEST AMPHITHEATER EVER BUILT.** It was built mainly as a place for people to watch fights between gladiators.

HISTORIANS ESTIMATE THAT ABOUT 500,000 PEOPLE AND 1 MILLION ANIMALS DIED IN THE ARENA.

The outer stone wall was built without mortar. Iron clamps—300 tons (272 T) of them—held it together.

TEMPLE OF KUKULCAN AT CHICHÉN ITZÁ

YUCATÁN PENINSULA, MEXICO

Construction: 800–900

The step pyramid is nearly **100 FEET (30 M)** tall. It was built with limestone, wood, and mortar.

The pyramid was built layer by layer. Ramps were used to help haul the limestone bricks up the pyramid.

THE PYRAMID HAS 365 STEPS, ONE FOR EACH DAY OF THE YEAR.

Twice a year when the sun sets, a **SHADOWY SNAKE** appears on the pyramid's side.

13

BURJ KHALIFA

DUBAI, UNITED ARAB EMIRATES

Construction: 2004–2010

Its tripod shape and a strong central core support its HEIGHT.

The Burj Khalifa is 2,717 feet (828 m) tall. It's the TALLEST STRUCTURE in the world.

The CENTRAL PINNACLE PIPE weighs 390 tons (348 T)!

WORKERS SPENT 22 MILLION HOURS BUILDING THIS WONDER!

WORLD FINANCIAL CENTER

SHANGHAI, CHINA

Construction: 1997–2008

The Shanghai World Financial Center looks like a BOTTLE OPENER!

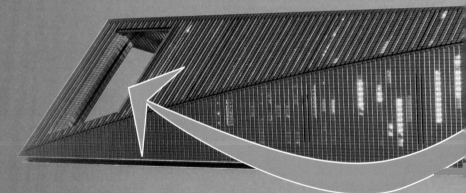

The open space at the building's top helps CUT DOWN WIND stress on the building.

The building boasts 101 floors above ground and 91 elevators.

PEOPLE CAN VISIT SOME OF THE TOP FLOORS TO GET A GREAT VIEW OF SHANGHAI.

KESHWA CHACA

Construction: around 1500

KESHWA CHACA is an Incan rope suspension bridge. It's more than 500 years old!

The bridge is made of **PLANT FIBER ROPES** and hangs almost 100 feet (30 m) above a river.

18

EVERY YEAR LOCALS BRING NEW ROPE TO REPLACE THE OLD.

The main walkway was made with **FOUR ROPES** and a mat of **SMALL TWIGS**.

19

TSING MA

HONG KONG, CHINA

Construction: 1992–1997

Tsing Ma is the LONGEST SUSPENSION BRIDGE that can handle trains.

Each tower was made with **71,650 TONS** (65,000 T) of concrete.

The bridge is designed to withstand the **STRONGEST WINDSTORMS**.

THE TOTAL LENGTH OF THE BRIDGE'S WIRE COULD WRAP AROUND THE WORLD FOUR TIMES!

MILLAU VIADUCT

MILLAU, FRANCE

Construction:
2001–2004

The Millau Viaduct is the **TALLEST VEHICLE BRIDGE** in the world.

IT WAS BUILT IN JUST **THREE** YEARS!

Its tallest point is **1,125 FEET** (343 m)—a bit taller than the Eiffel Tower.

IT TOOK WORKERS LESS THAN FOUR DAYS TO LAY DOWN 11,023 TONS (10,000 T) OF CONCRETE FOR THE BRIDGE DECK.

CRAB BRIDGE

Construction: 2012

CHRISTMAS ISLAND, AUSTRALIA

This bridge is for CRABS only.

CLEARANCE
5.5 m

Every year about 50 million crabs migrate across the island. They use the bridge to pass safely over a busy road.

THE BRIDGE'S SIDES ARE MADE OF STEEL MESH THAT THE CRABS CAN EASILY CRAWL UP.

BANFF NATIONAL PARK
ANIMAL CROSSING BRIDGES/TUNNELS

ALBERTA, CANADA

Construction: mid-1980s–present

Banff National Park has **SIX LAND BRIDGES** and **38 TUNNELS** built just for animals.

The bridges have trees, bushes, and grasses to make them more **forest-like.**

The bridges protect animals crossing a busy highway that runs through the park.

MOSQUE

Construction: 784–987

CATHEDRAL OF CÓRDOBA

CÓRDOBA, SPAIN

The Mosque Cathedral of Córdoba was built as a MOSQUE. Today it's a CATHEDRAL.

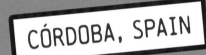

The dome was made by CRISSCROSSING RIBS to form arches.

The building's **DOUBLE ARCHES** allow it to have very high ceilings.

The building has **856 COLUMNS**. Most of them were taken from an **ANCIENT ROMAN** temple.

29

THE PIANO HOUSE

HUAINAN, CHINA

Construction: 2007

Architecture students designed this ONE-OF-A-KIND structure. The GLASS VIOLIN appears to lean against the GRAND PIANO.

ESCALATORS and a STAIRCASE inside the violin take VISITORS into the piano.

The piano makes a huge patch of **SHADE**. On sunny days, people **LOUNGE BENEATH** the piano.

The piano stands on three large, **CONCRETE PILLARS**. Space beneath the piano's open top is used as a **ROOFTOP PATIO**.

SANTA MARIA DEL FIORE (IL DUOMO)

Construction: 1296–1396

FLORENCE, ITALY

Il Duomo's dome is taller than the Statue of Liberty! It is the LARGEST STONE AND BRICK dome in the world.

Experts **STILL DON'T KNOW** how Filippo Brunelleschi was able to build the dome.

He invented a **SPECIAL HOIST** powered by oxen to help with construction.

MORE THAN 4 MILLION BRICKS WERE USED TO BUILD THE DOME!

UNDERGROUND CHURCHES OF LALIBELA

LALIBELA, ETHIOPIA

Construction:
1100–1300 (rough estimate)

All 11 underground churches were carved out of MASSIVE ROCKS.

To avoid flooding, builders dug a large system of canals and trenches.

First builders cut a general building shape from a huge rock. Then they carved out doors, windows, floors, and roofs.

SACSAYHUAMAN

CUSCO, PERU

Construction: around 1450

Sacsayhuaman was either an Incan fortress or a temple to the sun.

WORKERS CUT OR POUNDED ROCKS TO HAVE MOSTLY STRAIGHT LINES.

Large ropes, logs, levers, and hundreds of men hauled large boulders to the site.

To make the walls, workers fit **SHAPED LIMESTONE** boulders together like puzzle pieces.

Most rocks fit together TIGHTLY. Not even a sheet of paper can slide between them!

37

THE STATUE OF LIBERTY

Construction: 1876–1886

NEW YORK, NEW YORK, USA

The Statue of Liberty was a GIFT FROM FRANCE to the people of the United States.

Sheets of **24K GOLD** cover the statue's flame.

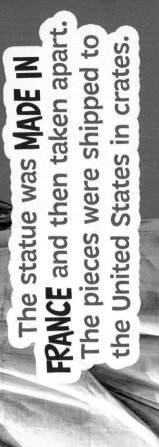

The statue was **MADE IN FRANCE** and then taken apart. The pieces were shipped to the United States in crates.

Workers used **SCAFFOLDING AND CRANES** to piece it back together.

The statue wears sandals—**SIZE 879**!

CHRIST THE REDEEMER

Construction: 1926–1931

RIO DE JANEIRO, BRAZIL

The statue stands **92 FEET (28 M) TALL**. It was built on a mountaintop **2,310 FEET (704 M)** above the city of Rio!

The statue's inner framework is made of **CONCRETE.**

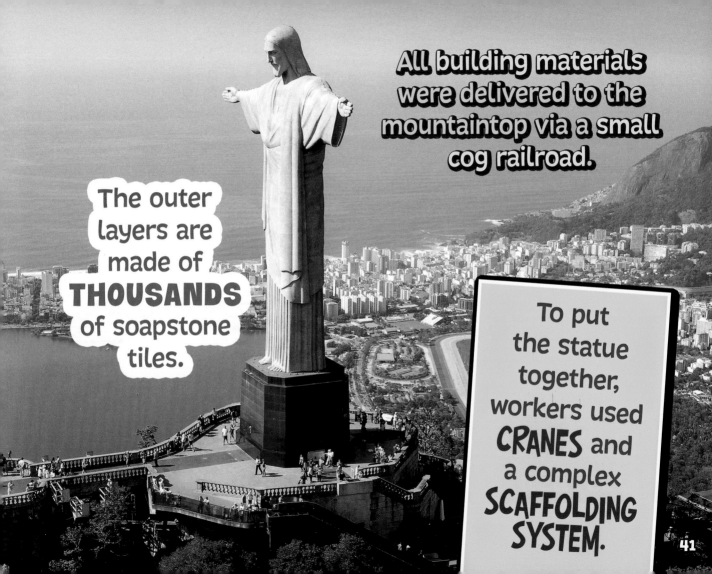

All building materials were delivered to the mountaintop via a small cog railroad.

The outer layers are made of **THOUSANDS** of soapstone tiles.

To put the statue together, workers used **CRANES** and a complex **SCAFFOLDING SYSTEM.**

MONTREAL BIOSPHERE

MONTREAL, CANADA

Construction: 1967

The 200-FOOT (61-M) TALL Montreal Biosphere was built for the 1967 WORLD'S FAIR. Today it's a museum.

WORKERS MADE THE FRAMEWORK BY WELDING TOGETHER STEEL TUBES TO FORM TRIANGLES.

They added 1,900 clear panels to make the building see-through.

NEW CENTURY GLOBAL CENTER

CHENGDU, CHINA

Construction: 2010-2013

Based on floor area, the New Century Global Center is the WORLD'S LARGEST building.

THREE U.S. PENTAGON buildings could fit inside it!

The 18-STORY SQUARE building was made using a GLASS and STEEL FRAME.

The building's GLASS ROOF has curves in it that look like RIPPLES.

A FAKE SUN inside the building shines 24 hours a day.

HABITAT 67

MONTREAL, CANADA

Construction: 1967

Habitat 67 was built to show a new kind of city living space.

The boxes were **MADE ON-SITE** in an assembly line way.

It's made from **354 STACKED** concrete boxes.

Once the boxes were made, they were insulated. Then **WINDOWS, KITCHENS, BATHROOMS,** and **ELECTRICAL SYSTEMS** were added.

A **CRANE** lifted each finished box to its **SPOT** on the stacked structure.

CATHEDRAL OF BRASILIA

BRASILIA, BRAZIL

Construction: 1958-1970

The Cathedral of Brasilia is a GEOMETRY lover's dream!

It is a **HYPERBOLOID** structure, meaning part of it **CURVES INWARD**.

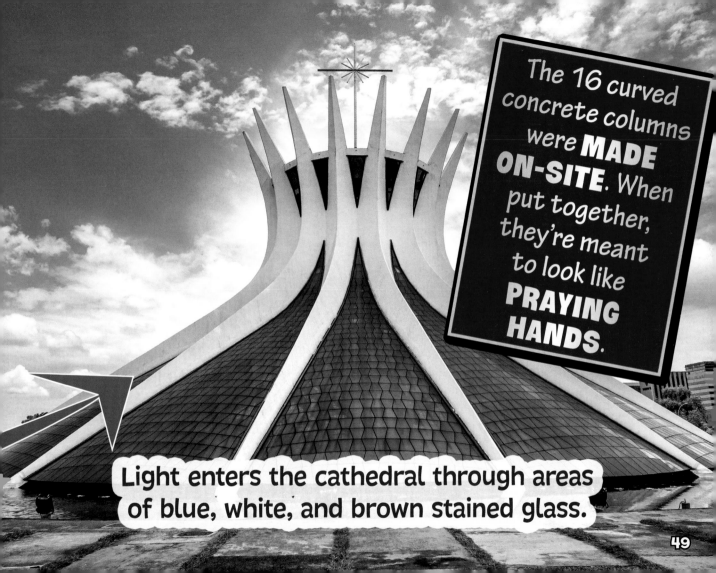

The 16 curved concrete columns were **MADE ON-SITE**. When put together, they're meant to look like **PRAYING HANDS**.

Light enters the cathedral through areas of blue, white, and brown stained glass.

NAKAGIN CAPSULE TOWER

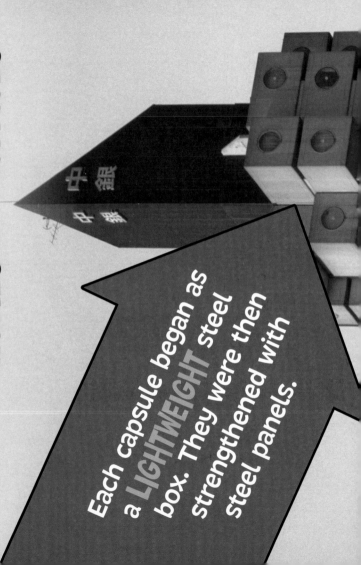

Construction: 1970-1972

TOKYO, JAPAN

THE CAPSULE TOWER IS MADE OF 140 CAPSULES THAT ARE USED AS **HOMES** AND **OFFICES**.

Each capsule began as a **LIGHTWEIGHT** steel box. They were then strengthened with steel panels.

The units were put into place using a **LARGE CRANE**.

The capsules **CAN BE REMOVED** or **ADDED** as needed.

51

SYDNEY
OPERA HOUSE

SYDNEY, AUSTRALIA

Construction:
1959-1973

The Sydney Opera House was ESTIMATED TO COST $7 million. Its actual cost was $102 MILLION!

The architect supposedly got his idea for the roof design from PEELING AN ORANGE.

The roof was built using 2,194 CONCRETE SECTIONS. The sections are held together with 217 miles (350 km) of STEEL CABLE.

53

BRUSSELS 1958 WORLD'S FAIR BUILDING: ATOMIUM

Construction: 1957-1958

BRUSSELS, BELGIUM

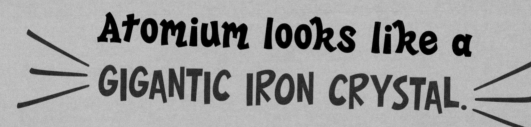

Atomium looks like a GIGANTIC IRON CRYSTAL.

It's made up of NINE 59-FOOT (18-M) stainless steel spheres.

HOLLOW TUBES CONNECT EACH SPHERE.

Visitors can go into the spheres and tubes to look out over the city.

BRUSSELS 1958 WORLD'S FAIR BUILDING: PHILIPS PAVILLION

Construction: 1958

BRUSSELS, BELGIUM

It housed an art and music exhibit that included about

350 SPEAKERS.

THE CURVED WALLS WERE MADE USING SAND MOLDS.

At the end of the fair, the building was TORN DOWN.

The building's UNIQUE SHAPE made art and music displays look and sound great!

BOSTON,
MASSACHUSETTS,
USA

Construction:
1795–1798

MASSACHUSETTS STATE HOUSE

Workers had to **FLATTEN BEACON HILL** by 50 feet (15 m) to get the **GROUND READY** for construction.

On July 4, 1795, **Samuel Adams and Paul Revere** placed the **keystone** for the building.

The original wooden dome **WAS COVERED WITH COPPER** in 1802. In 1874 it was covered with gold leaf.

The Massachusetts State House was the **TALLEST BUILDING** in Boston when it was completed.

HAGIA SOPHIA

ISTANBUL, TURKEY

Construction: 532-537

The church's **HUGE DOME** is 108 feet (33 m) across. It was the **LARGEST DOME** at the time it was built.

To keep the church space open, architects DID NOT USE PILLARS to support the dome. Instead, they used SPHERICAL TRIANGLE STRUCTURES called pendentives.

Materials came from **MANY PARTS** of the **WORLD**, including Greece, Egypt, and Syria.

Hagia Sophia has survived a **FIRE** and **EARTHQUAKES.** Its dome has partially collapsed several times.

CROOKED LITTLE HOUSE

SOPOT, POLAND

The idea for *this* UNUSUAL *building* came from FAIRY TALE ART.

WARPED WALLS, curved STAINED GLASS, and a SUNKEN ROOF give the building its crooked look.

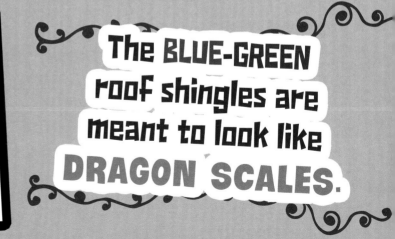

The BLUE-GREEN roof shingles are meant to look like DRAGON SCALES.

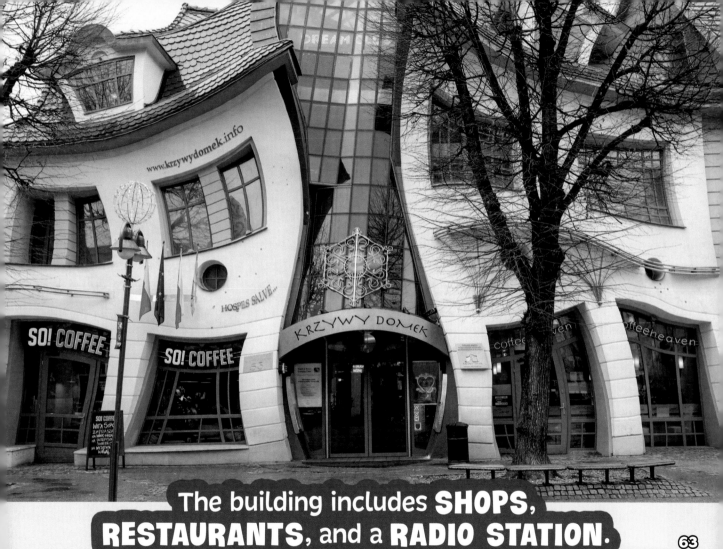

The building includes **SHOPS**, **RESTAURANTS**, and a **RADIO STATION**.

WALDSPIRALE
(FOREST SPIRAL)

DARMSTADT, GERMANY

Construction: 1998–2000

Germany's Forest Spiral apartment building climbs up, or **SPIRALS, 12 STORIES.**

It has more than **1,000 WINDOWS.** NO TWO ARE THE SAME.

All of the building's corners are **ROUNDED.**

The roof has **TREES, GRASS,** and **PLANTS** to feel like a **"FOREST."**

It was the first **BUILDING** in Germany to be built with **RECYCLED CONCRETE.**

NATIONAL CENTRE FOR THE PERFORMING ARTS (NCPA)

Construction: 2001-2007

BEIJING, CHINA

China's NCPA is called "THE EGG."

It is the **LARGEST** sky dome in the **WORLD!**

The shell is made of 18,000 titanium plates **and** 1,000 sheets of glass.

THE BUILDING WAS DESIGNED TO HONOR THE TRADITIONAL CHINESE SYMBOL OF HEAVEN AND EARTH.

AT&T STADIUM

ARLINGTON, TEXAS, USA

Construction:
2005–2009

AT&T Stadium is home to the NATIONAL FOOTBALL LEAGUE (NFL) team the Dallas Cowboys. It's the LARGEST NFL STADIUM ever built.

The stadium is almost 0.25 mile (0.4 km) long. It can seat up to 100,000 fans!

At 660,800 square feet (61,390 sq m), the stadium's roof is the largest RETRACTABLE ROOF in the world.

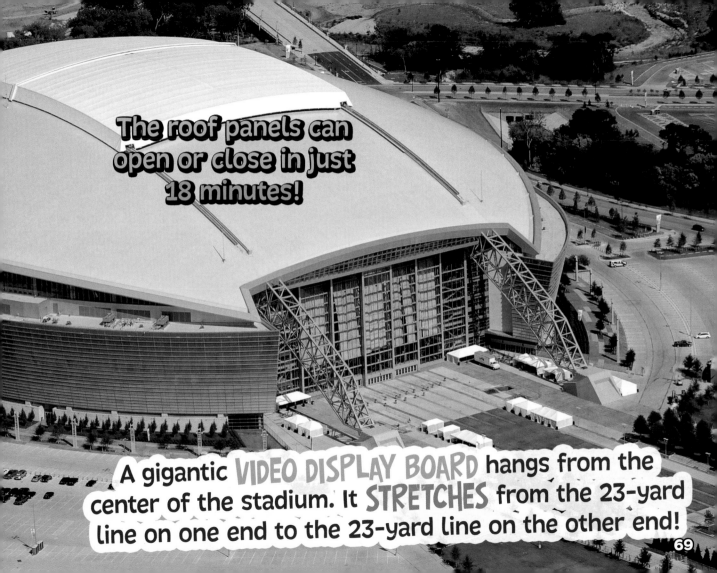

The roof panels can open or close in just 18 minutes!

A gigantic VIDEO DISPLAY BOARD hangs from the center of the stadium. It STRETCHES from the 23-yard line on one end to the 23-yard line on the other end!

ITAIPU DAM

PARAGUAY AND BRAZIL

Construction:
1975–1991

The Itaipu Dam is the **WORLD'S LARGEST** power plant.

The dam is 4.8 miles (7.7 km) long. It supplies **78 PERCENT** of Paraguay's **ELECTRICAL POWER.**

During construction, workers poured about 140 tons (127 T) of concrete every 20 minutes!

THE AMOUNT OF CONCRETE USED IN THE DAM IS ENOUGH TO BUILD 210 SOCCER STADIUMS!

PANAMA CANAL

PANAMA

Construction:
1907-1914

CREWS SET OFF 600 DYNAMITE EXPLOSIONS PER DAY!

240

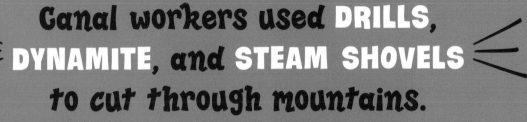

Canal workers used **DRILLS**, **DYNAMITE**, and **STEAM SHOVELS** to cut through mountains.

The Panama Canal allows ships to sail from NEW YORK to CALIFORNIA without going around South America.

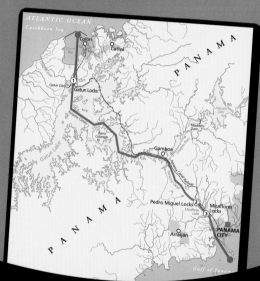

More than **25,000 WORKERS DIED** during the canal's construction.

KINGDA KA
ROLLER COASTER

SIX FLAGS GREAT ADVENTURE,
JACKSON, NEW JERSEY, USA

Construction: 2004–2005

Kingda Ka is
North America's
TALLEST, FASTEST
roller coaster.
It zooms up
45 STORIES
and reaches
128 miles
(206 km)
per hour.

FOUR CRANES were needed to keep up with BUILDING the coaster's track.

The track is 3,118 FEET LONG (950 M), but a ride takes only 50.6 SECONDS!

MONT SAINT MICHEL

NORMANDY, FRANCE

Construction: roughly 1000–1520 (several buildings)

According to legend, an **ANGEL** told a **BISHOP** to build a **MONASTERY** on the top of a mountain.

The **GRANITE** used to build it was transported from nearby islands **VIA BOAT**.

Construction of the buildings took **500 YEARS**!

Mont Saint Michel has **COLUMNS, SHARP SPIRES, SCULPTURES, ARCHES,** and **GARGOYLES.**

During very high tides, the **LAND BRIDGE** between mainland France and Mont Saint Michel is **COVERED WITH WATER.**

BUCKINGHAM
PALACE

LONDON, ENGLAND

Construction: Original House 1703 (various additions/changes in later years)

Buckingham was first built in 1703 as a townhouse for the **DUKE OF BUCKINGHA**

It became the **OFFICIAL R** residence in 1837.

QUEEN VICTORIA was the first monarch to live in the palace.

Today's Buckingham Palace ha **775 ROOMS**—78 are bathroor

The windows—all 760—are cleaned **EVERY SIX WEEKS**.

Construction: 1868–1884

SCHWANGAU, GERMANY

The castle is built **HIGH ON A RIDGE** and was King Ludwig II's **DREAM PALACE.**

NEUSCHWANSTEIN CASTLE

King Ludwig 11 was known as the "FAIRY TALE KING." He wanted his castle to look like it came out of a STORYBOOK.

Workers removed **26 FEET (8 M) OF ROCK** so the castle's base could be built.

The castle included all the **LATEST TECHNOLOGIES:** an electric bell system, central heating, and flushing toilets.

Neuschwanstein Castle was the **INSPIRATION** for **SLEEPING BEAUTY'S** Castle at Walt Disney World.

THE GLOBE

Construction:
original theater: 1599;
second theater: 1614;
modern reconstruction: 1997

TODAY'S GLOBE IS THE THIRD OF ITS KIND.
The first burned down
in 1613. The second was torn down
in 1644 to make room for housing.

Like the old Globe, the new Globe
is a **20-SIDED SHAPE**.

82

The **THATCHED ROOF** is made from 800 bundles of sedge (a grass-like plant).

Playwright WILLIAM SHAKESPEARE helped finance the original Globe.

GOAT HAIR was used in the Globe's plaster!

83

ST. BASIL'S CATHEDRAL

Construction: 1555–1561

The cathedral is famous for its **ONION**-shaped domes.

RED SQUARE, MOSCOW, RUSSIA

ST. BASIL'S CATHEDRAL was originally designed as **EIGHT CHAPELS** around a **central tower.**

St. Basil's is the most colorful cathedral in the world—both inside and out.

Builders created the domes by **HAND-PAINTING** metal sheets. Then they attached the sheets to **IRON FRAMEWORKS.**

GREAT WALL OF CHINA

CHINA

Construction:
220 BC–AD 1644

The Great Wall of China took about 1,800 YEARS to build.

It is
13,171 MILES
(21,197 km)
LONG!

The Great Wall was built to **PROTECT PEOPLE** and **LAND** from enemies.

It is not one wall. It's a **COLLECTION** of walls that span across mountains, valleys, plains, and desert.

STONE, BRICKS, SOIL, WOOD, STICKY RICE MORTAR, and SAND were used to make it.

About **400,000 PEOPLE DIED** while building the Great Wall. Many of them are **BURIED** in the walls.

CHAND BAORI

RAJASTHAN, INDIA

Construction: sometime between 800 and 900

Chand Baori is one of the **LARGEST STEPWELLS** in the world. It's 13 stories deep.

It was **BUILT** to **HOLD** rainwater.

The well has **3,500** perfectly symmetrical steps.

The **SQUARE** well has three sides of steps. The fourth side has **SCULPTURES**, **PILLARS**, and **BALCONIES**.

THE GREAT PYRAMID OF GIZA

The Great Pyramid was made as a **TOMB** for the Egyptian pharaoh Khufu.

It was originally **480 FEET (146 M) TALL.** Due to erosion it's now 455 feet (139 m) tall.

It is believed that **2.3 MILLION BLOCKS** were used in its construction.

Each **BLOCK** weighed about **2.5 TONS** (2.3 T) on average!

Experts think the **BLOCKS** were cut and put into place using sledges, rollers, and levers.

Scientists are still **UNSURE** of exactly how it was built.

MACHU PICCHU

NEAR CUZCO, PERU

Construction: around 1450

Machu Picchu was a **ROYAL ESTATE** built by the Inca.

It is a **MULTI-LEVEL CITY** with more than 150 buildings. Three thousand stone steps link them together.

The Inca came up with new methods to make their buildings stable during **EARTHQUAKES**.

They made walls stable by building doors and windows in a **TRAPEZOID** shape.

Workers cut **DRY STONES** and fit them together perfectly to construct the buildings.

ERICSSON GLOBE

Construction: 1986-1989

STOCKHOLM, SWEDEN

The Ericsson Globe is the **LARGEST SPHERICAL BUILDING** in the world.

It stands **262 FEET** (80 m) tall and houses a **16,000**-seat arena.

The Globe was made using **HOLLOW STEEL TUBES** that are connected with special joints.

Two **GLASS PODS** take visitors to the top in **16 MINUTES.**

The Globe's **COLOR CHANGES**, depending on the events inside. **RED** means a concert. **BLUE** means sports.

ST. VITUS CATHEDRAL

PRAGUE, THE CZECH REPUBLIC

St. Vitus Cathedral took almost **600 YEARS TO BUILD!**

The cathedral has three **STEEPLES**. The tallest one is about 329 feet (100 m) high.

Below the cathedral's altar is the **CRYPT**—a place where **IMPORTANT PEOPLE** are buried.

Legend says that **ROPES** made from a **PRINCESS' HAIR** lifted the biggest **BELL** into place.

The country's priceless **CORONATION JEWELS** lie within the cathedral behind two doors with **SEVEN LOCKS** each.

NOTRE DAME CATHEDRAL

PARIS, FRANCE

Construction: 1163-1345

More than 1,300 LEAD PLATES make up the roof of France's Notre Dame Cathedral.

So many trees were used to make the building that it got the nickname **"THE FOREST."**

Notre Dame's largest bell, the EMMANUEL BELL, weighs 13 tons (12 T). That's nearly as much as three average-sized AFRICAN ELEPHANTS!

PETRA

Construction: start unknown, but existed in 312 BC

Petra is a large, **ANCIENT CITY** in southern Jordan. It houses churches, altars, sculptures, and more than 800 tombs.

The tomb of King Aretas III (85–62 BC) reaches **MORE THAN 100 FEET (30 M)** from the canyon floor!

THE TOMB HAS COLUMNS AND DETAILED CARVED DECORATIONS.

Part of the city was built. Part was carved into rock.

The movie *INDIANA JONES AND THE LAST CRUSADE* was filmed at Petra.

LESHAN GIANT BUDDHA

NEAR LESHAN, CHINA

Construction: 713–803

The Leshan Giant Buddha was **CARVED** out of a **HILL**.

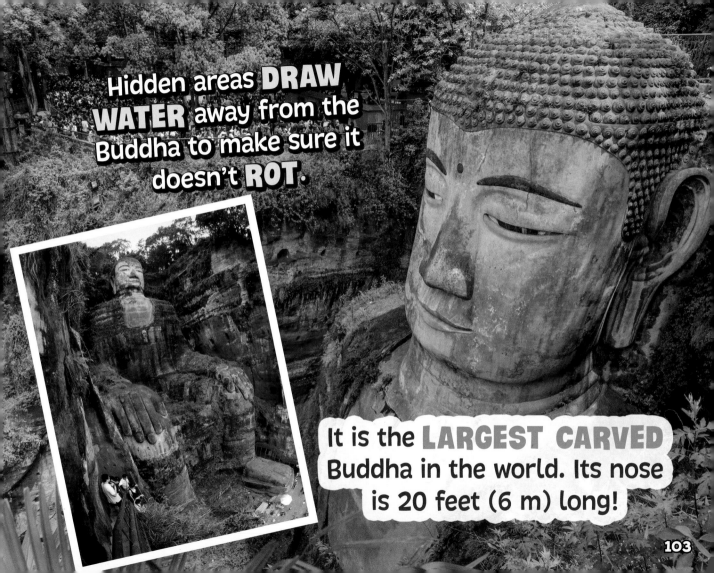

Hidden areas **DRAW WATER** away from the Buddha to make sure it doesn't **ROT**.

It is the **LARGEST CARVED** Buddha in the world. Its nose is 20 feet (6 m) long!

103

AAMI PARK

MELBOURNE, AUSTRALIA

Construction:
2006-2010

AAMI PARK IS A **SPORTS STADIUM** THAT CAN SEAT MORE THAN **30,000 PEOPLE.**

About **2,000** TRIANGULAR PANELS make up the 20 domes.

The roof frame is SELF-SUPPORTING—all the domes rely on each other to STAY PUT.

The domes collect RAINWATER for washing seats, flushing toilets, and watering the grass.

LEGO HOUSE

SURREY, ENGLAND

Construction: 2009

JAMES MAY BUILT A HOUSE IN ENGLAND WITH 3.3 MILLION LEGOS!

IT HAD A WORKING SHOWER AND TOILET.

NO ONE wanted to buy it, so it was **KNOCKED DOWN** in 2009.

BEIJING NATIONAL STADIUM

BEIJING, CHINA

Construction: 2003-2008

The Beijing National Stadium is often called the **"BIRD'S NEST."**

It was **BUILT** to **HOST** the 2008 Olympic Games.

It is the world's **LARGEST STEEL STRUCTURE**. It was crafted using 22.5 miles (36 km) of **UNWRAPPED STEEL**.

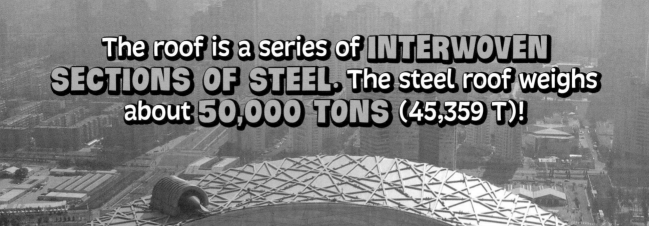

The roof is a series of **INTERWOVEN SECTIONS OF STEEL**. The steel roof weighs about **50,000 TONS** (45,359 T)!

GLOSSARY

amphitheater—a large, open-air building with rows of seats in a high circle around an arena

architect—a person who designs buildings and other structures

canal—a channel dug across land; canals connect bodies of water so ships can travel between them

cathedral—a large and important church

gargoyles—ugly human or animal figures used on buildings

Incan—belonging to the Inca, a group of Indian people in South America

legend—a story passed down through the years that may not be completely true

migrate—to move from one place to another

monastery—a place where men live and study to devote themselves to their religious vows

mosque—a place of worship for Muslims (people who follow the religion of Islam)

scaffolding—a temporary structure put up on the outside of a building

self-anchored—attached to oneself

span—the length between two supports, such as columns

sphere—a round solid shape, like a basketball or globe

stepwell—a deep water storage area lined with flights of stairs

suspension bridge—a walkway or roadway hung from two or more cables that are held up by towers

symmetrical—the same on both sides of a center line

thatched—made with straw or grass

viaduct—a long, raised roadway that's usually broken into many short spans

READ MORE

5,000 Awesome Facts 2: (About Everything!). National Geographic Kids. Washington, D.C.: National Geographic, 2014.

Morley, Jacqueline. *You Wouldn't Want to Be a Pyramid Builder!: A Hazardous Job You'd Rather Not Have.* You Wouldn't Want to Be. New York: Franklin Watts, an imprint of Scholastic Inc., 2014.

Pettiford, Rebecca. *Stadiums.* Amazing Structures. Minneapolis, Minn.: Jump!, Inc., 2016.

INTERNET SITES

FactHound offers a safe, fun way to find Internet sites related to this book. All of the sites on FactHound have been researched by our staff.

Here's all you do:

Visit *www.facthound.com*

Type in this code: 9781515747536

INDEX

Mind Benders are published by Capstone,
1710 Roe Crest Drive, North Mankato, Minnesota 56003
www.mycapstone.com

Editors: Jill Kalz and Megan Peterson
Designer: Veronica Scott
Media Researcher: Jo Miller
Production Specialist: Tori Abraham

Library of Congress Cataloging-in-Publication data is available on the Library of Congress website.
ISBN 978-1-5157-4753-6 (library binding)
ISBN 978-1-5157-4777-2 (paperback)
ISBN 978-1-5157-4785-7 (eBook PDF)
Summary: A collection of more than 100 facts about bridges, towers, buildings, and other structures around the world.

Photo Credits

Alamy: Douglas Lander, 95, Kohl-Photo, 97, Pulsar Images, 70; Dreamstime: lxuskmitl, cover (bottom); Getty Images: HADI ZAHER, 24; Glow Images: Deposit Photos, 63, ImageBROKER/Wigbert Rth, 19; iStockphoto: rmnunes, 49; Newscom: akg-images/Paul Almasy, 57, EPA/LARRY W. SMITH, 69, Europics, 31, PHOTOPQR/OUEST FRANCE, 77, Photoshot/UPPA/David Wimsett, 106, REUTERS/Yves Herman, 55, SIPA/CHINE NOUVELLE/GUO DAYUE, 109, ZUMAPRESS.com/Rob DeLorenzo, 74-75; Shutterstock: Adwo, 43, amadeustx, 36, Anton_Ivanov, 38-39, 89, aspen rock, 7, canadastock, 80, Chris Jenner, 72, Daniel Korzeniewski, cover (right), danmiami, 39 (inset), Dmitry Chulov, 35, Fabio Mancino Photography, 10, GNSKRW, 52, Gordon Bell, 58, Cloverz, 104, ID1974, 84-85, Ilona Ignatova, 14-15, Jeffrey M. Frank, 47, Jessmine, 32, LU JINRONG, 66-67, Luciano Mortula, back cover, (skyline), Mark Schwettmann, 41, Matej Kastelic, 28, Mikhail Markovskiy, 61, mumbojumbo, 22, Narongsak Nagadhana, 93, NathalieB, 99, Neil Mitchell, 78, Nightman1965, cover (top), Peter Hermes Furian, 73, Peter Stuckings, cover (left), 103, Pius Lee, 90-91, Pres Panayotov, 83, Pyty, 103, (inset), RestonImages, 13, Robert Crum, 26, Scotshot, 65, Sean Pavone, 86, sevenke, back cover (elephant), 3, Sira Anamwong, 5, structuresxx, 20, theowl84, 2, Vince Padilla, 9, vitmark, 92, volkova natalia, 101, Yu Zhang, 44, Zhoa jian kang, 16-17; SuperStock: Pantheon/ardea.com/Jean-Paul Ferrero, 25; UIG via Getty Images: Arcaid, 50-51

Design Elements by Capstone and Shutterstock

Printed in Canada.
010037S17